W9-DGG-566

Uncharted, Unexplored, and Unexplained

Scientific Advancements of the 19th Century

Robert Koch

and the Study of Anthrax

Mitchell Lane
PUBLISHERS

P.O. Box 196
Hockessin, Delaware
19707

HIGHLAND F

Uncharted, Unexplored, and Unexplained

Scientific Advancements of the 19th Century

Titles in the Series

Visit us on the web: www.mitchelllane.com
Comments? email us: mitchelllane@mitchelllane.com

Uncharted, Unexplored, and Unexplained

Scientific Advancements of the 19th Century

Robert Koch
and the Study of Anthrax

by Kathleen Tracy

Uncharted, Unexplored, and Unexplained

Scientific Advancements of the 19th Century

Copyright © 2005 by Mitchell Lane Publishers, Inc. All rights reserved. No part of this book may be reproduced without written permission from the publisher. Printed and bound in the United States of America.

Printing   1   2   3   4   5   6   7   8
    Library of Congress Cataloging-in-Publication Data
Tracy, Kathleen.
    Robert Koch and the study of anthrax / Kathleen Tracy.
        p. cm. — (Uncharted, unexplored & unexplained scientific advancements of the 19th century)
    Includes bibliographical references and index.
    Contents: A lethal weapon—A country doctor—An old adversary—A new age in medicine—The ultimate honor.
    ISBN 1-58415-261-3 (lib. bdg.)
    1. Koch, Robert, 1843–1910—Juvenile literature. 2. Microbiologists—Germany—Biography—Juvenile literature. 3. Anthrax—Juvenile literature. [1. Koch, Robert, 1843–1910. 2. Microbiologists. 3. Scientists. 4. Anthrax. 5. Nobel Prizes—Biography.] I. Title. II. Uncharted, unexplored & unexplained.
QR31.K6T3 2005
610'.92—dc22   2003024127

ABOUT THE AUTHOR: Kathleen Tracy has been a journalist for over twenty years. Her writing has been featured in magazines including *The Toronto Star*'s "Star Week", *Biography* magazine, KidScreen and *TV Times*. She is also the author of numerous biographies including "The Boy Who Would be King" (Dutton), "Jerry Seinfeld—The Entire Domain" (Carol Publishing), "Don Imus—America's Cowboy" (Carroll), "Mariano Guadalupe Vallejo," and "William Hewlett: Pioneer of the Computer Age," both for Mitchell Lane. She recently completed *Diana Rigg, the Biography* for Benbella Books.

PHOTO CREDITS: Cover, pp. 1, 3, 6, 10, 12, 18, 21, 26, 29, 34, 39, 40, 41—Corbis; pp. 22, 23, 24, 30, 32, 37, 38—Science Photo Library

PUBLISHER'S NOTE: This story is based on the author's extensive research, which she believes to be accurate. Documentation of such research is contained on page 47.

The internet sites referenced herein were active as of the publication date. Due to the fleeting nature of some web sites, we cannot guarantee they will all be active when you are reading this book.

Uncharted, Unexplored, and Unexplained

Scientific Advancements of the 19th Century

Robert Koch

and the Story of Anthrax

*For Your Information

In September and October 2001, letters containing anthrax powder were sent to several news organizations and public officials, setting off a national panic. In all, five people died from being exposed to anthrax sent through the mail. The perpetrator has never been caught. In the photo above, a college student is holding two petri dishes that contain cultures of the pathogen.

1

A Lethal Weapon

On September 19, 2001, a letter addressed to actress Jennifer Lopez was delivered to the offices of *The Sun*, a supermarket tabloid newspaper located in Boca Raton, Florida. Owned by American Media, which also publishes *The National Enquirer* and *The Globe*, *The Sun* specializes in intentionally exaggerated, wacky stories such as farm animals being abducted by aliens or sightings of mysterious creatures such as yetis (the so-called "abominable snowmen"). These stories aren't meant to be taken seriously. But the employees of the paper would soon find themselves in the middle of a deadly serious, real-life mystery.

When a mail clerk opened the letter addressed to Lopez, it was found to contain a Star of David and some strange, bluish-colored powder. The clerk showed the letter and its contents to several co-workers, including photo editor Robert Stevens. Stevens lightly sniffed at the powder to see if it had a distinguishing smell. Baffled but unconcerned, he put the letter out of his mind and looked forward to his upcoming vacation. He spent five days the following week visiting his daughter at her home in North Carolina.

On his last day there, Stevens began feeling sick. When he got home the next day, he felt worse. He spent the day in bed, assuming he must be coming down with a bad case of the flu. His condition steadily worsened. Early in the morning of October 2, he was rushed to the emergency room of John F. Kennedy Hospital in Atlantis, Florida. He was suffering from disorientation, a high fever, and vomiting. Stevens was so sick that he was unable to talk. To aid his breathing, doctors put him on a respirator as they tested him for meningitis, an inflammation of the brain caused by a virus or bacteria.

When Dr. Larry Bush looked in the microscope, what he saw shocked him. The rod-shaped bacilli, or bacteria, visible on the slide was anthrax, a potentially deadly disease that very rarely occurs in the United States. Dr. Bush quickly notified the Palm Beach County Health Department, which in turn contacted the Centers for Disease Control (CDC) in Atlanta, Georgia. The CDC, the leading federal agency for investigating out-breaks of diseases, immediately sent 12 investigators to track Stevens's movements to determine how he contracted the disease. Unfortunately, they weren't able to interview Stevens. He died on October 5 from complications related to anthrax infection.

Two days later, investigators discovered anthrax spores on Stevens's computer keyboard at work. His co-workers were tested. The testing revealed the presence of anthrax spores in the nasal passages of *The Sun*'s mail supervisor, Ernesto Blanco. At that point, authorities decided to test all employees in the building, requiring them to submit to nasal swabs and blood tests. Five more people tested positive for anthrax antibodies, meaning they too had been exposed. Although Blanco would develop anthrax symptoms and require hospitalization, he was fortunate enough to survive.

With the discovery of anthrax spores in *The Sun* mailroom and inter-views with employees who told them about the letter containing the strange powder, investigators began to put the pieces together. When they went to the Boca Raton post office, they discovered traces of anthrax spores there as well.

The investigation took another startling turn on October 12. An employee of NBC-TV in New York was also diagnosed with anthrax—two weeks after handling a letter addressed to Tom Brokaw that contained suspicious powder. Three days later, anthrax turned up yet again. This time it was in the offices of Senators Tom Daschle and Patrick Leahy in Washington, D.C.

In all, the anthrax attacks of September and October 2001 killed five people, including two postal workers, and sickened 19 others among the people who were exposed. Investigators would eventually determine that the anthrax-laced letters were mailed on September 18 and October 9 from a mailbox in Trenton, New Jersey. It would cost millions of dollars to clean up the affected government offices and postal facilities. Because the attacks happened in the immediate aftermath of September 11, immediate suspicion fell on foreign terrorists. The truth was apparently much closer to home.

All of the anthrax spores found in the letters were determined to be from the identical strain. That means they were all related and came from the same ancestor, just as you and all your cousins on your mother's side share the same grandmother. Specifically, that strain was the Ames strain that the U.S. military biodefense program—based in Frederick, Maryland—had used in its research. Because of this, the FBI and CDC believed the perpetrator was an American.

Although authorities questioned many people and in May 2003 found suspicious evidence—a box with holes that could accommodate protective biological safety gloves along with vials wrapped in plastic—in a pond near Frederick, no arrests were made.

Most officials believed the anthrax attacks were not related in any way to the terrorist attack on the World Trade Center, except for timing. A popular theory is that the perpetrator of the letters was a disgruntled scientist or government employee who wanted America to spend more time and money on its biodefense program. This program emphasizes research and development of new medical tools to protect civilians from bioterrorism—attacks against people using bacteria, viruses, or other germs.

Although the anthrax-letter attacks might seem like something out of science fiction and people were understandably afraid, the truth is that biological and germ warfare are nothing new. Pathogens—disease-causing organisms found in nature—have been used to destroy troops and civilian populations for centuries.

Anthrax has always been one of the favored pathogens. It is easy and inexpensive to make, and it can be stored almost indefinitely as a dry powder.

The British took advantage of these factors to devise a plan to devastate Germany during World War II. Called Operation Vegetarian, the idea was to infect cattle herds by dropping five million "anthrax cakes" from planes throughout the German countryside. Eventually the disease would spread from the herds to people. In wartime conditions with little or no access to antibiotics, it is estimated that millions of people would have died. The distribution of the cakes was scheduled to begin in the summer of 1944. When the invasion of Normandy on the coast of France proved successful and Allied troops had the German army on the run, Operation Vegetarian was canceled. The war was eventually won by conventional means. In late 1945, the British government destroyed the five million anthrax cakes. The story remained a secret until revealed in a *London Sunday Herald* article in 2001.

While anthrax as a weapon is feared, the organism itself played a valuable part in our understanding of both how germs can make us sick and how to find cures or preventions. In fact, anthrax was the first organism ever to be identified as a disease-causing agent. But when German scientist Robert Koch revealed his ground-breaking discovery, he never dreamed of the sinister uses that his findings would be used for one day.

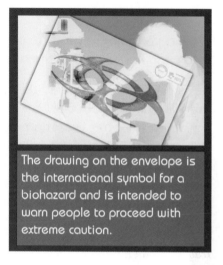

The drawing on the envelope is the international symbol for a biohazard and is intended to warn people to proceed with extreme caution.

Biological Warfare

1346: The first recorded use of using pathogens in battle occurred in what is now Feodosiya in the Crimean Peninsula of Ukraine. The city, then known as Kaffa, had been established as a colony of Genoa, Italy. Invading Tartar warriors besieged the city, but soon began dying of a plague. The survivors catapulted the dead bodies over the walls of the city. That infected the inhabitants, many of whom fled back to Italy while carrying the disease with them. Many medical historians believe this action started the "Black Death" epidemic that spread over the European continent.

Modern soldiers are trained how to survive a biological or chemical attack. Pictured above are some standard items given to British troops including the book *Survive to Fight*, a respirator—also commonly called a gas mask—gloves, syringes for taking medication to fight the effects of the attack, and pills that help prevent sickness in case of an attack.

1710: During a war between Russia and Sweden, Russian troops used the bodies of plague victims to transmit the disease to Swedish soldiers.

1767: During the French and Indian War, fought in North America between France and England, both sides relied heavily on their respective Indian allies. Twice the British attacked Fort Carillon, located in New York, and twice they were defeated. The English general Sir Jeffery Amherst gave Indians who fought for the French a gift of blankets, which had been infected with the smallpox virus. As a result, an epidemic killed many Indians. The next time the British attacked the fort, they won and renamed it Fort Ticonderoga.

1915: The first large-scale use of poisonous chlorine gas was by the Germans during the Second Battle of Ypres in April. They created a gas cloud that drifted over the trenches holding French and Canadian troops, resulting in many casualties. In addition to using chlorine, the Germans also developed grenades that carried bromide, a tearing agent, and mustard gas, which wasn't particularly lethal but caused agonizing blisters and blindness.

1917: When the United States entered World War I, German spies operating here reportedly infected horses and mules being exported to France with anthrax.

1988: At least 5,000 Kurds were killed in one hour in Halabja, a city in northern Iraq, when former Iraqi leader Saddam Hussein used chemical weapons to squelch civil unrest.

In the 19th century, scientists did not have the advanced technology we have today. The modest room pictured above was where Robert Koch set up his first lab. Because of his many discoveries, Koch is considered the father of bacteriology.

2

A Country Doctor

Robert Koch was born on December 11, 1843, in Clausthal, Germany, which is located in the Upper Harz Mountains. The region, in north-central Germany, had been an important mining area since the 10th century. Koch's father Hermann worked as a mine administrator to support his large family.

While his father put in long hours at his job, his mother Mathilde raised Robert and his 10 siblings. Robert, the third child, stunned his parents by announcing he had taught himself to read by poring over the local newspaper when he was just four years old. It was Hermann and Mathilde's first inkling that their son possessed a special intellectual gift. It was prophetic that young Robert's first toy was a magnifying glass, considering the fame he would one day achieve by studying objects far smaller than what the naked eye could see.

He began attending school at the age of five, and made rapid progress. By the time he was eight, he entered the local gymnasium, or secondary school. Robert showed an intuitive understanding of biology and was equally skilled at math. He also became an avid chess player.

Outside of the classroom, Robert often accompanied his uncle Eduard Biewend, who enjoyed studying nature and taking photographs. He inspired Robert to spend much of his free time in those activities.

Robert's ever-growing family eventually forced his father to buy a larger home. Still standing near the center of Clausthal, it housed two aunts, a cousin, and several servants in addition to the 13 immediate members of the Koch family.

Robert may have been his mother's favorite child. As biographer Thomas Brock points out, "Robert was apparently a real mother's joy. In addition to his passion for wildlife, he loved domestic plants and animals and took great pride, even as a nine-year-old, in decorating the house with flowers."[1]

It was time for Robert to leave home when he graduated from the gymnasium in 1862 at the age of 18. His two older brothers had moved to the United States, and his father wanted him to do the same thing to ease the family's financial burden.

Robert had other ideas. He wanted to attend the University of Göttingen, about 25 miles from Clausthal. Even though most of his grades at the gymnasium were good, there were some reservations. Brock notes that "His principal apparently had some doubt about Robert's ability to apply himself, however, as he emphasized that Koch's success would depend upon his ability to concentrate his energies on a chosen field of study."[2]

For a while after he entered the university, Robert wasn't sure where to concentrate his energy. His first choice was natural science, since this would enable him to join research expeditions to exotic foreign lands. But his family couldn't afford the expense of equipping him for such trips. Then he thought of becoming a teacher. Eventually, he decided to earn a medical degree. He studied under some notable scientists and researchers of the day, including Friedrich Gustav Jacob Henle. Two decades earlier, Henle had published the then-revolutionary theory that infectious diseases were caused by living microscopic organisms. While many in the scientific community dismissed such a notion, Koch was intrigued by the idea. It opened his mind to the possibility that humans were more affected by microorganisms—life forms far smaller than could be seen with the naked eye—than had previously been imagined.

His most significant accomplishment at the university came when he won a cash prize for a difficult anatomical study. The project took him nearly a year, and it was the first money he had earned on his own. His father was very pleased, especially since he had been providing the financial support for Robert's education.

When Robert graduated in 1866, he was faced with the necessity of earning a living. He couldn't depend on his father anymore. As a young boy, under the gray skies of Clausthal, Robert used to spend hours daydreaming about visiting other parts of the world. Now that he had his medical degree, he considered becoming a ship's doctor so he could sail to faraway places, such as the jungles of Africa, the great ports of Asia, or even the barren cold and snow of the Arctic.

There was one powerful reason to abandon that idea and stay closer to home. For several years, he had been in love with a young woman from Clausthal named Emmy Fraatz. Soon after graduating, he proposed to her and she accepted. But he needed a dependable source of income before he could marry Emmy.

His first job was as an assistant in the General Hospital of Hamburg. That didn't pay enough. The next opportunity was better. It was a clinic for retarded children in the village of Langenhagen.

"In this position, Koch would not only gain valuable experience, but he would be able to open up, on the side, his own private medical practice, thus making it possible for him to supplement his income," writes Brock. "He quickly became a popular doctor with the villagers and his medical practice flourished."[3]

Now he and Emmy could get married. Nearly the entire town of Clausthal turned out for the wedding. Robert seemed destined for a quiet career as a country doctor. Unfortunately, budget problems at the Langenhagen clinic squeezed out Robert just two years after he had started. He took several short-lived positions before finding a suitable opportunity in the town of Rakwitz, in the province of Posen, which is now part of Poland.

In the meantime, Emmy had given birth to the couple's daughter, Gertrud, on September 6, 1868. Gertrud would be their only child. She would also be one of the main reasons for Robert and Emmy to stay together, as strains in their relationship had already begun to appear.

In 1870, Koch volunteered as a field surgeon during the Franco-Prussian War. After his tour of duty was over, he returned home and passed the District Medical Officer's Examination. In 1872, he became the district surgeon for Wollstein, a farming district in then-Eastern Germany. Despite his busy schedule, Robert still managed to devote time to his many other interests, including archaeology, anthropology, and the newly emerging field of bacteriology. The latter science was of particular interest to Koch because of his association with professor Henle during his student days.

Determined to find out exactly what caused illness, Koch began his investigations. Because so many farm animals in his area were affected every year by anthrax, Koch focused on that disease, turning part of his four-room house into a working lab. Despite being isolated from other scientists and working alone, in just a few short years he would revolutionize our understanding of illness.

The Development FYI of the Microscope

When Koch started his research into pathogens—disease-causing organisms—he had only a few simple instruments. These included a homemade incubator and a microtome, a device for cutting thin slices of tissue. He also had a gift from his wife: a microscope. It would be his most valuable tool.

Nobody knows the identity of the first person who picked up a piece of curved glass, looked through it, and discovered that things appeared bigger. The oldest known lens was found in the ruins of ancient Nineveh and was made of polished rock crystal. Over time, people discovered that this crystal could focus sunlight and set fire to paper or fibers or dried leaves. There are references to magnifiers and "burning glasses" in the writings of the Roman philosopher Seneca, who lived in the first century A.D.

Centuries later, scientists began to apply the principles of magnification to their work. The earliest microscopes consisted of a tube with a holding plate at one end and a lens at the other end. They enlarged images by a factor of ten, or 10X. Insects, especially fleas, were a popular subject for viewing. As a result, early microscopes were often referred to as "flea glasses."

Around 1590, two Dutch spectacle makers, Zaccharias Janssen and his father Hans, discovered that they could greatly increase magnification by using more than one lens. This is called a compound microscope.

Anton van Leeuwenhoek

The man considered as the "father of microscopy" is Anton van Leeuwenhoek, who was born in Holland in 1632. He worked in a dry goods store that used magnifying glasses to count the number of threads in the cloth. He developed a way to grind and polish microscope lenses with a lot of curvature, which resulted in magnifications up to 270X. That allowed him to see a world previously too small to observe. He was the first to describe bacteria, yeast plants, and blood cells.

Leeuwenhoek made his microscopes out of silver and gold. After he died, his family sold them and they disappeared.

Early in his career Robert Koch worked as a district surgeon. But at night, he would spend hours in his lab, determined to discover the cause of illness. His most valuable tool was the microscope his wife Emmy gave to him.

3

An Old Adversary

Anthrax is one of the world's oldest known infections. Though it primarily affects grazing animals such as sheep, cattle, goats, and horses, it has also beleaguered humans for thousands of years. It is believed that anthrax was to blame for the fifth and sixth Egyptian plagues about 3,500 years ago. It was described both in the Old Testament and by the Roman poet Virgil. It was responsible for killing 40,000 horses and 100,000 cattle belonging to the Huns as they traveled across Eurasia in 80 A.D. It has variously been called black bain, charbon, murrain, splenic fever, and malignant pustule. Another name is woolsorters' disease, because of the high number of infections among people who worked close to livestock.

People can contract it in several different forms. By far the most common, accounting for about 95 percent of all cases, is cutaneous anthrax. It forms sores on the skin when contracted by methods such as contact with infected animals through a cut or by being bitten by flies. These sores are very dark in color and provide the source of the name anthrax. It comes from the Greek word *anthrakis*, which means coal. When treated with antibiotics, cutaneous anthrax is very rarely fatal. Untreated, it may kill up to 20 percent of its victims.

The rarest form of anthrax is gastrointestinal, which occurs from eating infected meat. Symptoms include abdominal pain, vomiting, and in severe cases, kidney malfunction. The deadliest form is inhalation anthrax. It often occurs in the textile industries among workers handling contaminated animal wool, hair, and hides. It is almost always fatal. This is the form that *Sun* photo editor Robert Stevens acquired.

While most people assume that preventing disease was the motivation for scientists trying to find a cure in the 19th century, those researchers had another pressing reason. There was an urgent desire to prevent the huge financial losses associated with decimated livestock in the farming areas of Europe.

"They had an economic interest in defeating anthrax, which was killing hundreds of thousands of livestock a year and ruining the food, textile, and leather industries dependent on animal products," said Boston College sociologist Jeanne Guillemin in a newspaper article published soon after the anthrax attacks. "They weren't worried about people. They were worried about the herds."[1]

By the time Koch turned his attention to anthrax, others before him had also researched it. In the mid-1800s, a British physician named John Bell noticed the relationship between anthrax and woolsorters disease. In 1863, Casimir-Joseph Davaine observed that microscopic rod-like bodies were inside infected sheep, but not inside healthy sheep. Five years later, he reported that blood taken from animals afflicted with anthrax and injected into healthy animals caused them to die. Yet nobody understood how the disease was truly caused and what part microorganisms such as bacteria might play in that illness.

Koch began his research by removing the spleens of infected carcasses, extracting some blood, then injecting it into healthy mice, using wood splinters as his homemade syringe. The rodents subsequently came down with anthrax, confirming that the disease could be spread via blood.

Koch developed this work further. For three years he spent all his spare time investigating whether or not anthrax bacilli that had never been in contact with any kind of animal could cause the disease. He obtained pure cultures of the bacteria by growing them in his house. In examining the cultures, he observed that under favorable conditions, the bacilli thrived and remained active. However, in unfavorable or inhospitable conditions such as drought, cold, or lack of oxygen, they produced spores that could survive these harsh conditions for years.

Koch understood why there might not be any instance of the disease for several years, then suddenly, seemingly out of nowhere, livestock would start dying. Because anthrax could take on the form of a spore, it could remain dormant, or in a kind of hibernation, for decades in a hostile environment. When conditions improved, it would become active again and start reproducing. Koch had uncovered the lifecycle of the anthrax bacilli.

With his new understanding, Koch successfully recovered spores, cultivated them in a pure culture, and then used these cultures in healthy animals to prove that the *bacillus anthracis* was the infecting agent. He proved that even though these pure cultures had had no contact with any animals, the bacilli could cause anthrax. In other words, he had discovered that germs were the causative agents of disease.

During Koch's time, people didn't understand why anthrax would seemingly appear out of nowhere. Koch discovered that bacillus anthracis could form a hard, protective coat around itself and take on the form of a spore. These spores could live in harsh conditions for many years then become active once the environmental conditions improved. Pictured above are vegetative anthrax bacteria.

Koch's work came to the attention of Ferdinand Cohn, a professor of botany at the University of Breslau. Impressed with the results, Cohn published Koch's findings in a botanical journal in 1876. Cohn also invited Koch to conduct a presentation in front of other professors and scientists. One of them was Julius Cohnheim, the director of the Institute of Pathology at the University of Breslau.

"This man (Koch) has made a magnificent discovery, which, for simplicity and the precision of the methods employed, is all the more deserving of admiration, as Koch has been shut off completely from all scientific associations," he said. "I regard this as the greatest discovery in the history of pathology, and believe that Koch will again surprise us and put us all to shame by further discoveries."[2]

Louis Pasteur is considered one of the greatest scientists of all time. He confirmed Koch's germ theory and went on to develop vaccines against anthrax and rabies. He also discovered that by applying heat to food, such as milk, it could be preserved longer. This process, called pasteurization, is used in many areas of the food industry.

As a result of this recognition and praise, Koch suddenly found himself a well-known researcher. Not everyone accepted his conclusions. In the minds of some scientists, Koch had not conclusively proven it was the bacillus and not some other unknown agent being injected into the animals. It wasn't until six years later that Koch's findings were finally verified by another renowned scientist, Louis Pasteur. As often happens in science, Pasteur built on Koch's findings to help prove that diseases of all kinds were caused by these agents.

It was literally a matter of life and death. At that time, a significant percentage of mothers who gave birth died soon afterward from what was called "childbirth fever." Authorities had no idea what caused the problem. Pasteur increasingly believed that the infection was being spread by physicians and hospital attendants from sick to healthy patients. He stressed to the doctors that to avoid infection it was necessary to avoid the germs.

In a famous speech before the Academy of Medicine in Paris, Pasteur said, "This water, this sponge, this lint with which you wash or cover a wound, may deposit germs which have the power of multiplying rapidly within the tissue. If I had the honor of being a surgeon not only would I use none but perfectly clean instruments, but I would clean my hands with the greatest care. I would use only lint, bandages, and sponges previously exposed to a temperature of 1300 to 1500 degrees."[3]

As Koch had discovered, it takes time for new theories to be accepted. Pasteur's ideas about antiseptics wouldn't be accepted for some time. However, he would soon prove beyond doubt his and Koch's belief about all disease being caused by microorganisms.

An electron micrograph of bacillus anthracis spores. Farm animals and people who work with them were at particular risk of contracting the disease because the spores would lie dormant in the soil. Louis Pasteur developed a vaccine against anthrax by injecting animals with a weakened form of the disease so that its body would produce antibodies. The antibodies would then protect the animal from contracting the disease in subsequent exposures.

Pasteur's experiment was actually rather simple. He put a drop of blood from a sheep dying of anthrax into a sterile culture and grew a culture. He repeated this procedure 100 times in order to dilute the original culture enough so that not a single molecule of the original culture remained in the final culture. Even so, the last culture grown by Pasteur was just as active as the first one. Since only the bacillus itself growing up in each new culture could manage not to be diluted, it proved once and for all that the anthrax bacillus and nothing else could be responsible for the disease. With this one experiment, the germ theory of disease was firmly established.

But that still didn't exactly explain how the disease spread in the fields. Farmers were often frustrated that live-stock grazing on one field were perfectly healthy while those in another area became sick and died. While the answer seems simple now, at the time it was a mystery. Pasteur used his powers of observation to gather the answer. One day while walking in a field, he noticed that the soil in certain parts of the field was a different color. He learned that the farmer had buried some sheep that had died from anthrax in the areas where the soil was lighter. He realized the color change was due to earthworms aerating, or churning up, the soil as they fed on the sheep carcasses. As they ate, they brought anthrax spores up to the surface, thereby spreading the disease to the sheep grazing in the field.

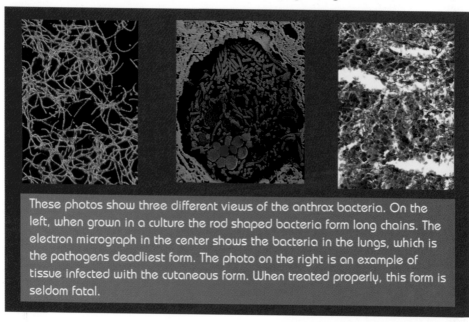

These photos show three different views of the anthrax bacteria. On the left, when grown in a culture the rod shaped bacteria form long chains. The electron micrograph in the center shows the bacteria in the lungs, which is the pathogens deadliest form. The photo on the right is an example of tissue infected with the cutaneous form. When treated properly, this form is seldom fatal.

Armed with the knowledge that he and Koch had amassed, Pasteur set out to develop an anthrax vaccine. He weakened the strength of the bacillus by heating it. When he injected the weakened anthrax into an animal, the animal's body produced enough antibodies in response to keep it from getting sick when exposed to a full strength anthrax bacillus. Pasteur demonstrated his vaccine on a farm outside Paris in 1881 by vaccinating 25 sheep out of a flock of 50. The other 25 were not given any protection. Then he administered a powerful dose of anthrax to the entire flock. Every one of the sheep that had not been vaccinated died. All of the vaccinated sheep survived.

Although it was Pasteur who would get the credit for developing the vaccine for anthrax, it would not have been possible without Koch having unraveled the life cycle of the anthrax bacillus.

During the time that Robert Koch was practicing medicine, great advances were being made in both the understanding of illness and its treatment. But many people were skeptical of the new methods. They preferred to rely on folk medicine that had been passed down in families or cultures for generations. Below are some remedies and cures used to combat sickness before the advent of modern medicine.

Scarlet fever: Feed a baked onion to the patient.

Whooping cough: Place the head of the sick child into a hole in a meadow for a few minutes at dusk. Or put three earthworms and the wooden chips from three pump handles in a bag and tie it around the child's neck.

Tuberculosis: Smoke dried cow dung in a pipe.

Cold: Rub a mixture of goose grease and turpentine on the patient's chest.

Teething: Apply leeches behind the infant's ears.

Cough and sore throat: Tie a small piece of pork to a string and dangle it down the patient's throat. Repeat as needed.

Mental illness: Immerse sufferers in the sea until they nearly drown. Then take them to church and say a mass over them.

Baldness: Take grass that grows near nine wells. Cook it in water taken from the same nine wells, and then drink the concoction. As the grass grows back, so will the person's hair.

Warts: Rub the wart with peas, and then throw the peas into a well. Or rub the wart with a potato and bury the potato afterward.

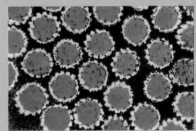

Warts are caused by the Human Papilloma Virus, pictured above.

One of the more important tools used by Robert Koch was photo-micrography. In order to document his findings as thoroughly as possible, he would take pictures of the images he saw under his microscope. Koch pioneered the technique, which soon became a widely adopted practice by other scientists such as Dr. L. Bendikson, who is shown here using ultra-violet light to make his photomicrographs.

4

A New Age in Medicine

Despite the new-found notoriety that his discovery of the anthrax bacillus had generated, Koch returned to his position in Wollstein and spent the next four years doing additional research and study of bacteria. In 1877 he published an important paper on the investigation, preservation, and photographing of bacteria. In the paper, he described the method he developed of taking thin layers of bacteria and fixing them by heat onto glass slides, then taking pictures of them. These pictures were called photomicrographs, and Koch pioneered the technique. He also invented the tools and the procedure for culturing microorganisms in a drop of solution on the underside of a glass slide, called the hanging drop technique.

The following year, Koch conducted experiments on the etiology, or cause, of wound infection. He was able to identify the germ that caused septicemia, or blood poisoning. Even though infected blood contained the septicemia germ, it wasn't visible under a microscope. He knew that other scientists would be skeptical of his results. So he set about figuring out a way to visibly show that his results were correct. Through trial and error, he discovered that staining the septicemia germ with methyl violet dye caused it to show up under a microscope. He then photographed the germs so that people outside of his laboratory could see them.

Koch also kept investigating which bacteria were causing which disease. By infecting animals with materials from different things, he produced six different types of infections, with each one caused by a specific microorganism. Then he transferred the infections into different animals, and he successfully reproduced the original six infections. In the same study, he found that the bodies of animals, including people, are extremely hospitable environments for the development of bacteria. He published these findings in 1878, providing the rest of the scientific community with his carefully notated experiments.

The techniques he developed for conducting experiments would greatly influence the way many other scientists carried out their experiments. These techniques became known as Koch's postulates (theories). Each of these postulates must be satisfied before it can be accepted that particular bacteria cause particular diseases.

1. The agent must be present in every case of the disease.

2. The agent must be isolated from the host and grown in a lab dish.

3. The disease must be reproduced when a pure culture of the agent is injected into a healthy susceptible host.

4. The same agent must be recovered again from the experimentally infected host.

Even with all his discoveries, Koch was limited in his research because he was still working out of his small home in Wollstein. That would soon change. As a result of his experiments and papers, Koch was now considered one of the great research scientists of his day. In 1880 he was appointed as a member of the Imperial Health Institute in Berlin. When he arrived at his new job, he was extremely disappointed and frustrated to discover his new workspace was a narrow room that was hardly better than his home-made lab. Eventually, however, he was moved to a more spacious area that better suited his needs. Along with a team of assistants, Koch tackled the problem of how to cultivate bacteria outside the body of a host to make research easier. He needed to find some kind of medium, or substance that could support bacterial life, on which he could contain and grow his deadly bacteria.

At first, he used the tissue from sheep's eyes, but he wanted something that didn't rely on animal carcasses. He experimented with all kinds of growth mediums and nutrient baths. Nothing worked exactly the way he wanted. Then he learned that the wife of one of his research associates used a gelatin-like substance called "agar agar"[1] to make her jellies and jams more solid in summer. Something immediately clicked in his brain and he knew that was the solution. Koch's lab assistant, J. R. Petri, designed a special shallow, circular dish to hold the agar medium and bacteria samples so they would be easy to work with. Called Petri dishes, they are still used in labs all over the world.

By most accounts, Koch could be difficult to work with and took personal offense if anyone disagreed with his conclusions. He also had a big ego and frequently felt he was competing with other scientists, especially Pasteur. Part of the rivalry was reflected in national politics. Pasteur was French, while Koch was German. In the late 19th century, those two countries were frequently at political odds with one another.

To make it easier to grow his bacteria cultures, Koch had one of his assistants, J. R. Petri, design a special dish to hold a gelatin-like substance called agar. Today, the Petri dish is used in every lab the world over. The anthrax pictured above is growing on agar in a Petri dish.

It was almost as if the scientists represented national pride. Each time Pasteur announced a new finding, Koch felt compelled to try and go one better, for both his personal reputation and the honor of Germany. With the mysteries of anthrax pretty much solved, he turned his intellect to one of the deadliest diseases afflicting humans. This was tuberculosis, often referred to as TB or "the great white plague."

As Koch wrote in 1882, "If the number of victims which a disease claims is the measure of its significance, then all diseases, particularly the most dreaded infectious diseases, such as bubonic plague, Asiatic cholera, etc., must rank far behind tuberculosis. Statistics teach that one-seventh of all human beings die of tuberculosis, and that, if one considers only the productive middle-age groups, tuberculosis carries away one-third and often more of these."[2]

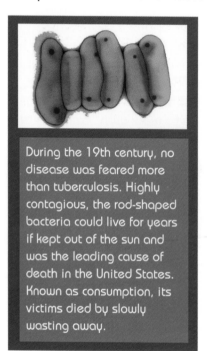

During the 19th century, no disease was feared more than tuberculosis. Highly contagious, the rod-shaped bacteria could live for years if kept out of the sun and was the leading cause of death in the United States. Known as consumption, its victims died by slowly wasting away.

In general, the primary symptom of tuberculosis is a chronic lung infection that causes fever, wracking coughs, weight loss, and night sweats. The tubercle bacilli—the bacteria that caused the disease—could grow in any of the body's organs and in the process cause severe damage or even destroy the organ completely. Eventually, many of those infected literally waste away and die.

Tuberculosis is highly contagious. The tightly packed conditions of rapidly growing cities in the latter part of the 19th century provided ideal conditions for the spread of the disease. It wasn't uncommon for whole families to be wiped out.

It is primarily spread through the air by coughing or sneezing, though it could also be carried in milk and other foods. Another means of transmission is through human saliva. Starting in the 1880s, many cities passed laws prohibiting spitting in public.

The knowledge that human saliva could contain the deadly germ led to changes in behavior. For example, "The amazing discovery that bacteria could survive in spit for an entire day even convinced many women to stop wearing their long, trailing dresses into town for fear they might pick up sputum and drag it into their homes."[3] A well-known poster of the era showed a handsome young man holding a handkerchief delicately against his mouth, rather than spitting on the ground. These precautions were important, as the tuberculosis bacillus is a hardy microbe. As one medical website notes, "Direct sunlight will kill TB in a few minutes, but in dark, dusty environments, it can live for up to 20 years."[4]

Although it was known that tuberculosis was due to an infective agent, the organism had not yet been isolated and identified. Unlike the large anthrax bacillus, the tuberculosis germ was much smaller. Finding it was that much more difficult. However, Koch modified his method of staining and was able to identify the bacillus and reveal the true nature of the disease.

An unexpected obstacle arose. Koch had difficulty growing the organism in pure culture. Eventually, he succeeded in isolating the organism on a succession of media. On March 24, 1882, he announced in front of the Physiological Society of Berlin that he had isolated and grown the tubercle bacillus. Koch believed that this particular bacterium was the causative agent for all forms of the dreaded disease. Scientists around the world confirmed his findings. Once again, Koch was hailed for his discovery.

"What electrified the world was not the scientific splendor of the achievement, but rather the feeling that man had finally come to grips with the greatest killer of the human race," wrote medical researchers Rene and Jean Dubos. "In Europe and America Koch became the pope of medical science. In Japan a new shrine was erected to him, as to a demigod."[5]

This discovery had another benefit. The excitement generated by his work inspired many young scientists to become "microbe hunters," as early bacteriologists were called. Using the same methods as Koch, they began seeking causes and cures for other diseases. Almost overnight, there was hope that diseases that had once seemed invincible could now be prevented by developing vaccines based on Koch's work. For the first time in recorded history, it appeared that mankind had microbes on the run.

31

Polio cells

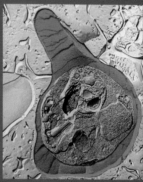
Malaria cells

Cholera cells

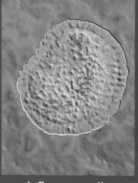
Influenza cells

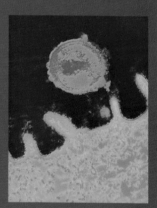
Diptheria cells

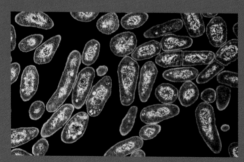
Tuberculosis cells

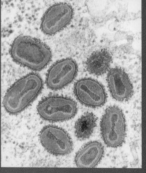
Smallpox cells

Before the widespread use of vaccines and antibiotics, the possibility of contracting a deadly disease was very high, particularly among children. Here are some of the most dreaded diseases that researchers such as Koch were working to prevent or cure.

Polio: A horribly debilitating disease that attacks the spinal cord and brain. Victims would often become paralyzed. There is still no cure for polio but thanks to the vaccine developed by Dr. Jonas Salk in the 1950s, polio has been virtually wiped out in developed countries.

Malaria: Also called ague, the symptoms include fever, chills, aches and pains, nosebleeds, and a cough. It was eventually discovered that malaria was spread by infected mosquitoes.

Cholera: One of the deadliest diseases at that time, it was spread through contaminated water. The more severe strains of cholera were frequently fatal, with symptoms including spasms, chills, vomiting, and terrible thirst.

Influenza: A highly infectious viral illness that infects the respiratory tract and often led to pneumonia and death. The first recorded pandemic, or world-wide epidemic, was in 1580. At least four pandemics of influenza occurred in the 19th century, while the influenza pandemic of 1918–1919 killed over 40 million people.

Diphtheria: A very common and very contagious disease—especially among children, among whom it was a leading cause of death—it was identified by fever, physical weakness, and a thick dark-colored membrane that forms in a patient's throat. This membrane resulted in breathing difficulties, and it was known as el garitillo (the strangler) in Spanish. The disease often weakened its victims' hearts and many of them died of heart failure. Many people believe diphtheria is the disease that killed George Washington in 1799.

Tuberculosis: Frequently referred to as "consumption," it was the leading cause of death in the United States during the last part of the 19th century and early 20th centuries. Death was caused by the patient slowly wasting away.

Smallpox: For centuries, smallpox was among the most feared diseases in the world. It was almost always fatal to children and the elderly. The virus that caused smallpox resulted in frightening-looking pustules, or blisters, that covered the victim's face and nearby soft tissues. Sometimes these pustules became so swollen that it was extremely difficult to breathe.

Koch's identification of the causative agents of disease enabled other scientists to develop treatments. Nobel Prize winner Emil von Behring, pictured above, developed the first anti-toxin that could help to destroy the poison spread by bacteria in the blood stream. He proved it was possible to treat diphtheria by injecting animals with the blood serum of another animal infected with the disease. This treatment was called serum therapy.

5

The Ultimate Honor

In 1883, Egypt experienced a severe outbreak of cholera. There was grave concern that the disease would spread to Europe. Hoping to prevent a disastrous epidemic, the German government asked Koch to interrupt his work on tuberculosis and join a government commission being sent to Egypt to investigate the disease. Once there, Koch set to work identifying the causative agent. Within a relatively short period of time, he believed he had isolated a comma-shaped bacillus as the specific cause of cholera. Ironically, his efforts were stymied because the outbreak ended. But the trip still yielded positive results. Koch was able to discover the cause of amoebic dysentery and the bacilli of two varieties of Egyptian conjunctivitis, a painful eye condition.

Wanting to complete his work on cholera, Koch traveled to India, where cholera was contagious. That means it was always present in this particular region. There he identified the cholera microorganism and revealed it was transmitted mostly via drinking water. It could also be spread in food and even on clothing. From these findings, Koch formulated rules—which are still used today—to help control cholera epidemics, particularly the conservation of water supplies. For his work he was rewarded with 100,000 German marks by the government. The money allowed Koch the freedom to increase his research.

Flush from this success, Koch resumed his tuberculosis research. With his feathers a bit ruffled from all the acclaim that had recently been bestowed on Pasteur for his discovery of the anthrax vaccine, Koch sought to develop a treatment for tuberculosis. He discovered that the disease could be cured in its early stages by inserting dead and alive, or inactive and active, bacilli into animals. Encouraged by this finding, he then tried to make a curing agent. In 1890, Koch used a sterile liquid produced from cultures of the bacilli, called tuberculin, as the active agent.

Tuberculin would be Koch's most notable failure and most embarrassing professional moment. Before he had tested its effectiveness thoroughly, he announced that it would prove to be a cure. His optimism proved to be premature. In subsequent experiments, tuberculin proved to be ineffective in curing the disease. It did have some value, however. It became a useful tool in the diagnosis of tuberculosis.

The setback did little to tarnish his lifelong body of work. In 1891 he was appointed the head of Berlin's Institute for Infectious Diseases, which attracted researchers from all over the world to study the new science of bacteriology. Today the Institute is known as the Robert-Koch-Institut and is comparable to America's Centers for Disease Control and Prevention, the national center for disease research and prevention.

During his years running the Institute, Koch remained active in his research. He frequently traveled to remote areas in Africa and India to investigate an assortment of exotic diseases, including leprosy, rinderpest, bubonic plague, surra, and Texas fever. Along with British bacteriologist Ronald Ross, Koch concluded that malaria was transmitted by mosquitoes. He also advanced the theory that typhus—another deadly disease—was transmitted directly person to person, as opposed to the then-popular conventional wisdom that it was spread in water. That new understanding allowed public health officials to establish control measures that aided in lowering instances and spread of the disease.

During this time, there was a major change in his personal life. His marriage with Emmy ended in divorce in 1893. Several years earlier, he

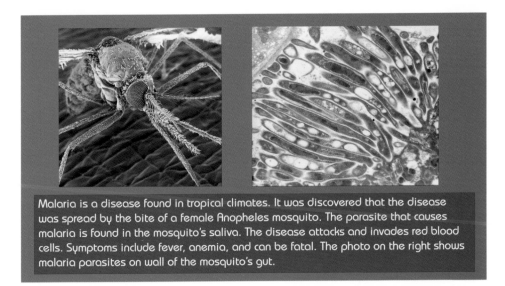

Malaria is a disease found in tropical climates. It was discovered that the disease was spread by the bite of a female Anopheles mosquito. The parasite that causes malaria is found in the mosquito's saliva. The disease attacks and invades red blood cells. Symptoms include fever, anemia, and can be fatal. The photo on the right shows malaria parasites on wall of the mosquito's gut.

had met a young woman named Hedwig Freiburg and he married her soon after his divorce. Hedwig was courageous. Robert had tested tuberculin on himself, but suffered a severe reaction. To prevent him from having to go through any more pain, she volunteered to undergo further testing.

Hedwig apparently provided another benefit for her husband. As writers Meyer Friedman and Gerald Friedland point out, "His lifelong, wistful desire to visit strange and exotic countries took on an irresistible attraction after his new marriage. Thus, from 1893 until his death in 1910, Koch journeyed almost continuously to different parts of Africa and India, seeking out possible means of eradicating sleeping sickness, cholera, malaria, and intractable infections that killed cattle and sheep."[1]

Like ripples spreading out from a stone thrown into a pond, Koch's methods resulted in great strides against other diseases from people with whom he worked.

"Koch was surrounded by an enthusiastic group of dedicated workers," writes Thomas Brock. "How did Koch manage to pull together this marvelous and effective group so rapidly? Not through force of

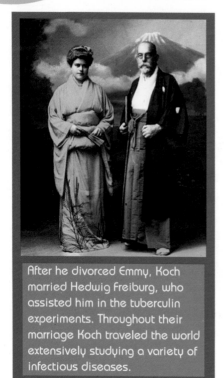

After he divorced Emmy, Koch married Hedwig Freiburg, who assisted him in the tuberculin experiments. Throughout their marriage Koch traveled the world extensively studying a variety of infectious diseases.

personality or an insistence on obedience, but through example. No one worked harder than Koch, and his example drove the others of his group forward with him. Sitting at his microscope, surrounded by his colleagues, daily making new and exciting discoveries: this was the way Koch led his group."[2]

One of best examples of his influence is illustrated by the fight against diphtheria. Using Koch's methods, Friedrich Loeffler identified the specific bacteria that caused diphtheria. But what intrigued researchers more was why the disease seemed to affect the victim's heart. They eventually concluded that the bacilli produced poisonous toxins—or poisonous substances—that entered the bloodstream and damaged the heart tissue as it passed through.

Using this information, two of Koch's colleagues—Emil von Behring and Shibasaburo Kitasato—grew diphtheria bacteria and strained out the bacilli. Only a solution containing the toxin remained. When they injected guinea pigs with large doses of the solution, it killed them. When they injected the rodents with small doses, the animals came down with a mild case of diphtheria but recovered. Once the guinea pigs were healthy, they were given another small dose of the toxin. This time, they did not get sick at all.

Next, blood taken from a guinea pig that had diphtheria was mixed with toxin. The blood-toxin mixture was then injected into a healthy guinea pig, which again remained disease free. The healthy animal did not become sick because the infected blood acted as an antitoxin. When the antitoxin was injected into a guinea pig that already had

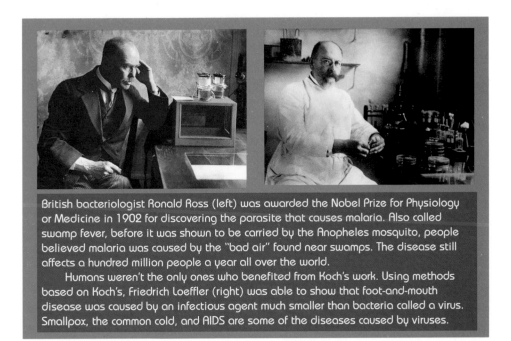

British bacteriologist Ronald Ross (left) was awarded the Nobel Prize for Physiology or Medicine in 1902 for discovering the parasite that causes malaria. Also called swamp fever, before it was shown to be carried by the Anopheles mosquito, people believed malaria was caused by the "bad air" found near swamps. The disease still affects a hundred million people a year all over the world.

Humans weren't the only ones who benefited from Koch's work. Using methods based on Koch's, Friedrich Loeffler (right) was able to show that foot-and-mouth disease was caused by an infectious agent much smaller than bacteria called a virus. Smallpox, the common cold, and AIDS are some of the diseases caused by viruses.

diphtheria, the animal was cured. The antitoxin both prevented and cured the disease.

The next step was to prove that the animals' blood had developed immunity to the disease. Blood from one of the guinea pigs that had recovered from the mild case of diphtheria was mixed with toxin. This mixture was administered to a healthy animal, which did not get sick. More importantly, when blood from the animal that had recovered from the mild case of diphtheria was injected into an animal that was already sick with the disease, the second animal was cured. This meant the blood-toxin mixture acted as an antitoxin that could both prevent and cure the disease.

Another Koch associate, Paul Ehrlich, developed methods of making the antitoxin in large quantities and gauging the amount that each patient would need. This monumental breakthrough, based on Koch's work, led to the cure for diphtheria which has saved the lives of countless people. For their work with diphtheria and other diseases, both Behring and Ehrlich won Nobel Prizes.

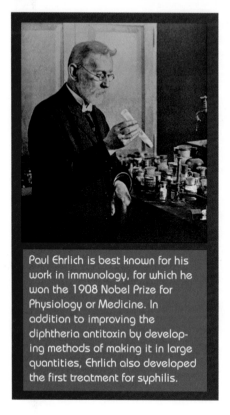

Paul Ehrlich is best known for his work in immunology, for which he won the 1908 Nobel Prize for Physiology or Medicine. In addition to improving the diphtheria antitoxin by developing methods of making it in large quantities, Ehrlich also developed the first treatment for syphilis.

So did Robert Koch. Ironically, even though tuberculin had been his professional low point, Koch was awarded the Nobel Prize for Medicine in 1905 for his work on tuberculosis. In his acceptance speech, Koch urged governments to invest the necessary support to fight the disease.

"We should not close our eyes to the fact that the fight against tuberculosis needs quite considerable financial resources," he said. "Basically it is only a question of money. The more free beds for consumptives that are endowed in well-equipped and well-run sanatoria and nursing-homes, the more adequately the families . . . are supported, so that the sick are not dissuaded from going into hospital out of concern for their relatives, and the more social welfare centres are set up, the more rapidly will tuberculosis decrease in importance as a wide-spread infectious disease."[3]

Five years later, at the age of 66, Robert Koch died of a heart attack in Baden-Baden on May 27, 1910. His ashes rest in an urn in the west wing of the Robert-Koch-Institut in Berlin.

He was not universally beloved. As Brock notes, "Robert Koch began his scientific career as an eager amateur, stealing a few hours away from his medical practice in order to experiment with bacteria and disease. He ended his career as an imperious and authoritarian father figure whose influence on bacteriology and medicine was so strong as to be downright dangerous. . . . Early in his career, no one would have predicted that this hard-working and eager young researcher would turn into a crusty and opinionated tyrant."[4]

After identifying the pathogen that caused tuberculosis, a cure remained elusive. Koch's belief that inoculating patients with tuberculin, as shown here, would cure the disease proved unfounded. It wasn't until the development of antibiotics that an effective treatment was found.

Koch was awarded the 1905 Nobel Prize for Medicine, pictured here, for his work on tuberculosis. When accepting the award, he urged governments to financially support the work of scientists.

Despite this, Robert Koch's single-minded determination in pursuing his research will never be forgotten. "In discovering the little animals that caused anthrax, and the little animals that caused tuberculosis, Koch founded the science of bacteriology," write Friedman and Friedland. "Of one thing we are certain: we shall forever be indebted to the general practitioner of Wollstein."[5]

Alfred Nobel

The Nobel Prizes are the world's most prestigious international awards. They are the brainchild of Alfred Nobel, a Swedish chemist and engineer who invented dynamite. Nobel had intended for his explosive invention to be a controllable tool that made blasting rock and the construction of canals and tunnels a relatively safe process. He became deeply distressed when some nations began using dynamite as a weapon of war. In his will, he left his nine million dollar fortune to establish annual awards "to those who, during the preceding year, shall have conferred the greatest benefit on mankind."[6]

His will also specified that two Nobel groups be formed. The one based in Stockholm, Sweden, chooses the award winners in science, literature, and economics. The second, located in Oslo, Norway, chooses the winner of the peace prize. It's believed that Nobel chose Norway to give the peace prize because Norwegians had a reputation among Europeans for finding peaceful solutions to international problems.

Nobel's family members were shocked when they learned that Alfred had given away his estate. They contested his will. But their efforts to keep the money failed and the first awards were distributed in 1901 to honor achievements in physics, chemistry, medicine, literature, and peace. The Nobel Prize for Economics was added in 1968.

Here are the Nobel Prize winners who shared honors with Koch in 1905.

Chemistry: Adolf von Baeyer (Germany) worked on organic dyes and hydroaromatic compounds.

Physics: Philipp Eduard Anton von Lenard (Germany) discovered many of the properties of cathode rays during his research.

Literature: Henryk Sienkiewicz (Poland) was most famous for Quo Vadis, a novel that depicted the persecution of the Christians in Rome during the reign of the Emperor Nero.

Peace: Baroness Bertha Sophie Felicita von Suttner (Austria) was an author who promoted disarmament and peace among European countries.

Chronology

1843	Born on December 11 in Clausthal, Germany
1848	Reads to his parents from a newspaper
1852	Enters gymnasium
1862	Enters University of Göttingen
1866	Graduates from University of Göttingen as a doctor
1867	Marries Emmy Fraatz
1868	Daughter Gertrud born
1870	Serves in a battlefield hospital during the Franco-Prussian war
1872	Becomes district medical officer in Wollstein; begins to experiment with microbes
1873	Starts to study anthrax
1876	Discovers the anthrax-causing microorganism
1877	Takes first photographs of bacteria
1880	Appointed to the Imperial Health Institute in Berlin
1882	Isolates tuberculosis bacillus
1883	Leads team of German researchers to Egypt to try to discover the cause of cholera
1884	Isolates the cholera bacillus
1885	Appointed professor of hygiene at the University of Berlin
1890	Develops tuberculin, which fails as a cure for tuberculosis but can be used to test for the disease
1891	Appointed director of the new Institute for Infectious Diseases
1893	Marries Hedwig Freiburg
1896	Conducts research in South Africa
1905	Wins the Nobel Prize for Medicine
1910	Dies on May 27 in German health resort of Baden-Baden

Timeline of Discovery

1796	English physician Edward Jenner introduces a smallpox vaccine.
1807	Oliver Evans invents the conveyer belt.
1812	Napoleon's surgeon, Baron Larrey, develops a painless method of amputation.
1816	Théophile René Laënnec of France invents the stethoscope.
1829	Louis Braille perfects his reading method for the blind.
1842	American surgeon Crawford Long performs the first surgical operation using anesthesia.
1846	Elias Howe invents the sewing machine.
1857	Louis Pasteur publishes the results of his experiments with fermentation.
1859	Charles Darwin writes *The Origin of Species*.
1869	Dmitri Mendeleyev produces the Periodic Table of the Elements.
1876	Alexander Graham Bell invents the telephone.
1879	Thomas Edison invents the incandescent light bulb.
1885	Louis Pasteur tests his rabies vaccine on humans for the first time.
1887	Sherlock Holmes, the famous fictional detective created by Arthur Conan Doyle, appears for the first time in the novel *A Study in Scarlet*.
1888	George Eastman introduces the Kodak hand-held camera with the slogan "You press the button, we do the rest."
1895	Wilhelm Roentgen discovers X-rays.
1899	The Bayer Company patents aspirin and begins selling it commercially.
1901	The first Nobel Prizes are awarded.
1918	A worldwide influenza pandemic kills more than 40 million people in six months.
1929	Alexander Fleming discovers penicillin.
1944	Selman Waksman discovers streptomycin, which is used against tuberculosis.
1953	Francis Crick and James Watson describe the double helix shape of DNA.
1955	Jonas Salk announces the development of his polio vaccine.
1979	The World Health Organization declares that smallpox has been officially eradicated.
2003	An outbreak of SARS (Severe Acute Respiratory Syndrome) in China raises fears of a worldwide pandemic.
2004	In China, one man has died and 35 others are infected by an outbreak of anthrax.

Chapter Notes

Chapter 2   A Country Doctor

1. Thomas D. Brock, *Robert Koch: A Life in Medicine and Bacteriology* (Washington, D.C.: ASM Press, 2000), p. 8.
2. Ibid., pp. 9–10.
3. Ibid., p. 15.

Chapter 3   An Old Adversary

1. Peter Gorner, "From Bible to battlefield, anthrax has widespread past," *Chicago Tribune*, October 21, 2001.
2. Thomas D. Brock, *Robert Koch: A Life in Medicine and Bacteriology* (Washington, D.C.: ASM Press, 2000), pp. 46–47.
3. Dr. David Cohn, "The Life and Times of Louis Pasteur," http://www.labexplorer.com/louis_pasteur.htm

Chapter 4   A New Age in Medicine

1. According to Graham R. Kent, Senior Instructor of Laboratories of Biological Sciences at the University of Massachusetts, the word agar comes from the Malay word "agar agar" meaning jelly.
2. Selman Waksman, *The Conquest of Tuberculosis* (Berkeley, CA: The University of California Press, 1964), p. 20.
3. Visual Culture—Infectious Disease—Tuberculosis, http://www.nlm.nih.gov/exhibition/visualculture/tuberculosis.html
4. Tuberculosis in Indonesia, Prevention and Treatment, http://www.expat.or.id/medical/tuberculosis.html
5. Waksman, p. 92.

Chapter 5   The Ultimate Honor

1. Meyer Friedman and Gerald W. Friedland, *Medicine's 10 Greatest Discoveries* (New Haven, CT: Yale University Press, 1998), pp. 63–64.
2. Thomas D. Brock, *Robert Koch: A Life in Medicine and Bacteriology* (Washington, D.C.: ASM Press, 2000), pp. 92–93.
3. Robert Koch—Nobel Lecture: The Current State of the Struggle against Tuberculosis, http://www.nobel.se/medicine/laureates/1905/koch-lecture.html
4. Brock, p. 5.
5. Friedman and Friedland, p. 64.
6. Nobel e-museum, http://www.nobel.se/literature/

Glossary

anthrax (ANN-thracks)—the first disease-causing bacteria to be discovered.

bioterrorism (by-oh-TERR-ehr-izm)—an attack using germ warfare or the intentional release of a toxin or biological agent.

cutaneous (cue-TAY-nee-us)—relating to the skin.

etiology (eh-tee-ALL-oh-gee)—study of the cause or origin of a disease.

infectious disease (in-FECK-shus dis-EEZ)—an illness that is passed from one person to another.

influenza (in-flew-EHN-zuh)—a viral respiratory tract infection; also called the flu.

medium (MEE-dee-uhm)—a nutrient system for the artificial cultivation of cells or organisms, especially bacteria.

pathogens (PATH-oh-jenz)—organisms that cause disease.

Petri dish (PEA-tree dish)—shallow, cylindrical dish made of plastic or glass with a cover, used for tissue cultures and to hold solid media for culturing and sub-culturing bacteria.

plague (PLAYG)—a serious, contagious bacterial infection that kills large numbers of people.

septicemia (sep-tuh-SEE-mee-uh)—an invasion of the bloodstream by virulent microorganisms from a local seat of infection accompanied especially by chills, fever, and prostration.

spore (SPOR)—dormant, environmentally resistant microorganism that can develop into a new individual.

Star of David symbol associated with the Jewish religion, comprised of two connected triangles.

For Further Reading

For Young Adults

Aaseng, Nathan. *The Disease Fighters: The Nobel Prize in Medicine*. Minneapolis, MN: Lerner Publications Company, 1987.

Farrell, Jeanette. *Invisible Enemies: Stories of Infectious Disease*. New York: Farrar Straus Giroux, 1998.

Ramen, Fred. *Epidemics: Deadly Diseases Throughout History—Tuberculosis*. New York: The Rosen Publishing Group, Inc., 2001.

Snedden, Robert. *Scientists and Discoveries*. Chicago: Heinemann Library, 2000.

Works Consulted

Brock, Thomas D. *Robert Koch: A Life in Medicine and Bacteriology*. Washington, D.C.: American Society for Microbiology Press, 1999.

Brock, Thomas D. *Milestones in Microbiology*. American Society for Microbiology Press, 2d edition, Washington, D.C., 1998.

Friedman, Meyer and Gerald W. Friedland. *Medicine's 10 Greatest Discoveries*. New Haven, CT: Yale University Press, 1998.

Gorner, Peter. "From Bible to battlefield, anthrax has widespread past." *Chicago Tribune*, October 21, 2001.

Jakab, E.A.M. *Louis Pasteur: Hunting Killer Germs*. New York: McGraw-Hill/Contemporary Books, 2000`` `.

Koch, Robert. K. Codell Carter (translator). *Essays of Robert Koch*. Westport, CT: Greenwood Press, 1987.

Waksman, Selman. *The Conquest of Tuberculosis*. Berkeley, CA: The University of California Press, 1964.

On the Internet

Nobel e-Museum—Medicine 1905
http://www.nobel.se/medicine/laureates/1905

Robert Koch (1843-1910)
http://german.about.com/library/blerf_koch.htm

Other Remedies of "Folk Medicine"
http://www.enoreo.on.ca/socialstudies/pioneer-virtual/folkmed.html

Visual Culture—Infectious Disease—Tuberculosis
http://www.nlm.nih.gov/exhibition/visualculture/tuberculosis.html

Tuberculosis in Indonesia, Prevention and Treatment http://www.expat.or.id/medical/tuberculosis.html

ABCNEWS.com—Timeline of Germ Warfare
http://abcnews.go.com/sections/nightline/DailyNews/timeline_biowar.html

Varner, Gary R. "Sacred Water: Faeries, Healing, Warts and Dreams"
https://www.authorsden.com/visit/viewarticle.asp?AuthorID=1215&id=11373

Anthrax
http://ajedrez_democratico.tripod.com/Operation-Vegetarian.htm

Kaufmann, Steffan H.E. "Historical Perspective: Robert Koch's highs and lows in the search for a remedy for tuberculosis."
http://www.nature.com/nm/special_focus/tb/historical_perspective/historical_perspective.htm

Questions and Answers About Anthrax
http://www.bt.cdc.gov/agent/anthrax/faq/index.asp

Robert Koch—advancing the field of bacteriology
http://www.iah.bbsrc.ac.uk/schools/scientists/KOCH.htm

LabExplorer.com—The Life and Times of Louis Pasteur by Dr. David Cohn
http://www.labexplorer.com/louis_pasteur.htm

Britannica Guide to the Nobel Prizes—Koch, Robert
http://www.britannica.com/nobel/micro/325_28.html

Anton Van Leeuwenhoek—Biography of Anton Van Leeuwenhoek
http://inventors.about.com/library/inventors/blleeuwenhoek.htm

Common Diseases of the 19th Century
http://www.enoreo.on.ca/socialstudies/pioneer-virtual/diseases.html

Index